Original Artwork © 1999 Susan Winget
Text Copyright 1999

The Brownlow Corporation
6309 Airport Freeway
Fort Worth, Texas 76117

ISBN:1-57051-4070
Printed in China

Dear Teacher

Illustrated by
Susan Winget

Brownlow

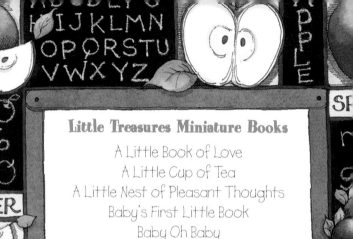

Little Treasures Miniature Books

A Little Book of Love
A Little Cup of Tea
A Little Nest of Pleasant Thoughts
Baby's First Little Book
Baby Oh Baby
Beside Still Waters - Catch of the Day
Dear Daughter • Dear Teacher
For My Secret Pal

Friend • Grandmother
Grandmothers Are for Loving
Happiness Is Homemade
Mom, I Love You
My Sister, My Friend
Quiet Moments of Inspiration
Seasons of Friendship
Sister • Tea Time Friends
They Call It Golf

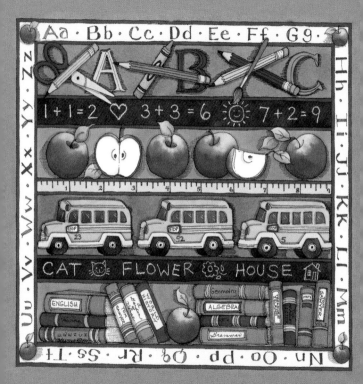

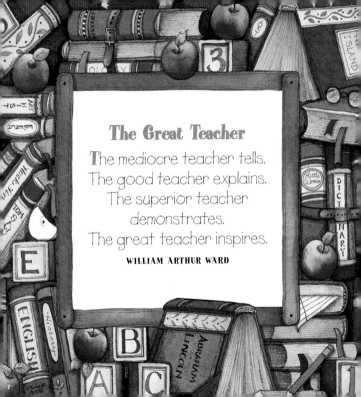

The Great Teacher

The mediocre teacher tells.
The good teacher explains.
The superior teacher
demonstrates.
The great teacher inspires.

WILLIAM ARTHUR WARD

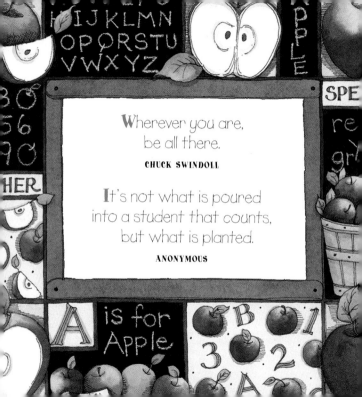

Wherever you are,
be all there.

CHUCK SWINDOLL

It's not what is poured
into a student that counts,
but what is planted.

ANONYMOUS

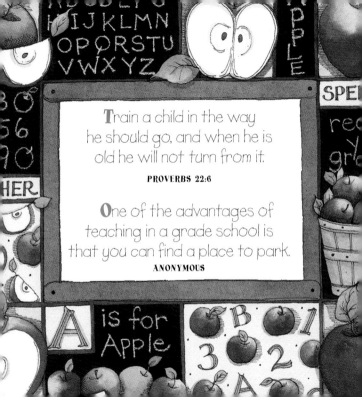

Train a child in the way
he should go, and when he is
old he will not turn from it.

PROVERBS 22:6

One of the advantages of
teaching in a grade school is
that you can find a place to park.

ANONYMOUS

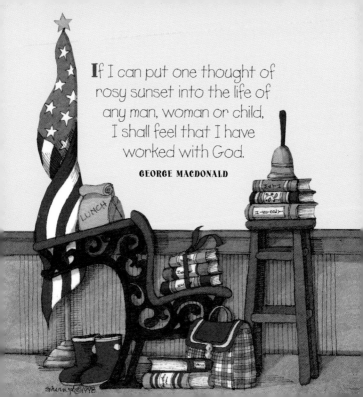

If I can put one thought of rosy sunset into the life of any man, woman or child, I shall feel that I have worked with God.

GEORGE MACDONALD

A O B ✶ C ✶ D ◉ E 🐘 F ✿ G

Give a little love to a child
and you get a great deal back.

JOHN RUSKIN

Children love to learn
but hate to be taught.

ANONYMOUS

✏ 1 ⭐ 2 🐤 3 🌸 4 ♥♥ 5

A B C D E F G

A teacher affects eternity;
no one can tell where his influence stops.

HENRY ADAMS

Everyone is ignorant, only
on different subjects.

WILL ROGERS

The art of teaching is
the art of assisting discovery.

MARK VAN DOREN

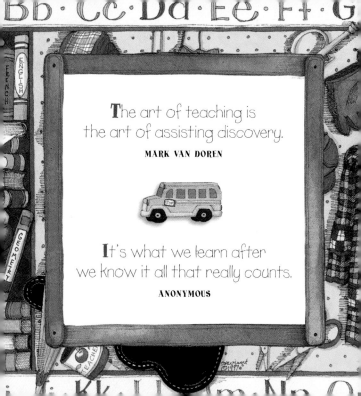

It's what we learn after
we know it all that really counts.

ANONYMOUS

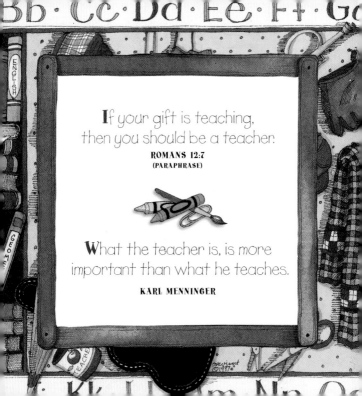

If your gift is teaching,
then you should be a teacher.

ROMANS 12:7
(PARAPHRASE)

What the teacher is, is more
important than what he teaches.

KARL MENNINGER

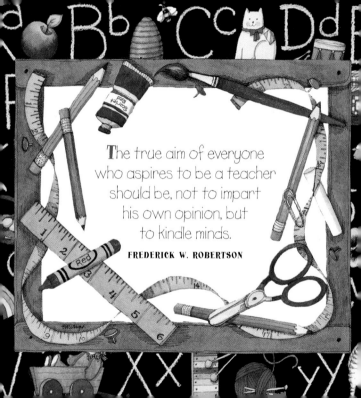

The true aim of everyone who aspires to be a teacher should be, not to impart his own opinion, but to kindle minds.

FREDERICK W. ROBERTSON

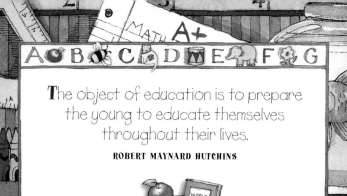

The object of education is to prepare
the young to educate themselves
throughout their lives.

ROBERT MAYNARD HUTCHINS

Nothing you ever do
for children is ever wasted

GARRISON KEILLOR

Let us always be open to
the miracle of the second chance.

DAVID STIER

The man who can make
hard things easy is the educator.

RALPH WALDO EMERSON

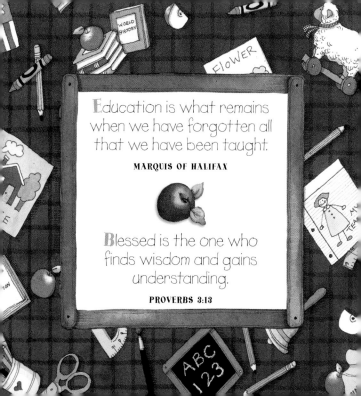

Education is what remains when we have forgotten all that we have been taught.

MARQUIS OF HALIFAX

Blessed is the one who finds wisdom and gains understanding.

PROVERBS 3:13

There are three things to remember when teaching: know your stuff; know whom you are stuffing; and then stuff them elegantly.

LOLA MAY

Don't let failure go to your head.

HAIM GINOTT

A B C D E F G

The Teacher's Psalm

The Lord is my teacher. I shall not want. He maketh me to learn in God's out-of-doors. He teacheth me by his written word. He instructeth my soul. He guideth me in the paths of true knowledge for his name's sake. Yea, when the day's task is done, and life's lessons have been learned, I will fear no evil. For thou wilt be with me, my Teacher and my Comforter still. Thou teachest even my enemies to become pupils of the Great Teacher. Thou leadest me gently from the known to the unknown. Thou givest me satisfaction in my day's work. Surely goodness and mercy shall follow me all the days of my life, and I shall be a learner in the school of the Great Teacher forever.

FREDERIC S. GOODRICH

1 2 3 4 5

Carve your name on hearts
and not on marble.

CHARLES H. SPURGEON

What we hope ever to do with ease,
we must learn first to do with diligence.

SAMUEL JACKSON

The object of teaching a child
is to enable him to get along
without his teacher.

ELBERT HUBBARD

Teaching that impacts
is not head to head,
but heart to heart.

HOWARD G. HENDRICKS

After finishing a unit on France, the teacher mentioned that the word "yes" was "oui" and pronounced "wee" in French. A girl raised her hand and said, "well in English 'wee' means going down a slide."

The one thing worse than
a quitter is the person who
is afraid to begin.

ANONYMOUS

A Teacher's Prayer

Lord, who am I to teach the way
To little children day by day,
So prone myself to go astray?

I teach them knowledge but I know
How faint they flicker and how low
The candles of my knowledge glow.

I teach them love for all mankind
And all God's creatures, but I find
My love comes lagging far behind.

Lord, if their guide I still must be,
Oh let the little children see
The teacher leaning hard on Thee.

LESLIE P. HILL

From the very beginning of his education, the child should experience the joy of discovery.

ALFRED NORTH WHITEHEAD

All a child's life depends on the ideal it has of its parents. Destroy that and everything goes—morals, behavior, everything. Absolute trust in someone else is the essence of education.

E.M. FORSTER

Children will usually obey if you explain patiently what you want them to do— and stand over them while they do it.

ANONYMOUS

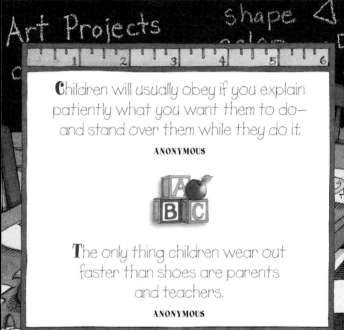

The only thing children wear out faster than shoes are parents and teachers.

ANONYMOUS

The wildest colts make
the best horses.

ANCIENT PROVERB

Children have more need of
models than of critics.

JOSEPH FOUBERT

It is deviant behavior for an adolescent to be pleasant.

PEGGY GOLDTRAP

Children are messengers we send to a time we will not see.

ANONYMOUS

Teachers get the best from their students when... they give the best of themselves.

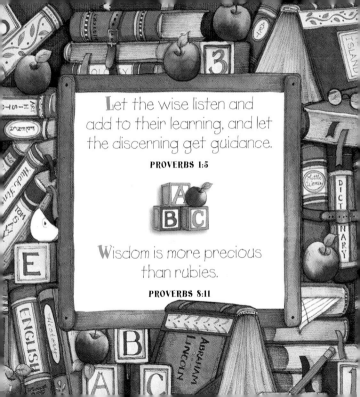

The entire object of true education is to
make people not merely to do the right things,
but to enjoy them; not merely industrious,
but to love industry; not merely learned,
but to love knowledge; not merely pure,
but to love purity; not merely just,
but to hunger and thirst after justice.

JOHN RUSKIN

A B C D E F G

A young child, a fresh unicuttered mind, a world before him—to what treasures will you lead him?

GLADYS M. HUNT

Men occasionally stumble over the truth, but most of them pick themselves up and hurry off as if nothing happened.

WINSTON CHURCHILL

1 2 3 4 5

A B C D E F G

This world belongs to the person
who is wise enough to change his mind
in the presence of the facts.

ROY L. SMITH

The wise carry their knowledge
as they do their watches—not for
display but for their own use.

ANONYMOUS

1 2 3 4 5

The cure for boredom is curiosity. There is no cure for curiosity.

ANONYMOUS

Whoever walks with the wise grows wise

PROVERBS 13:20

The people who influence you
are people who believe in you.

HENRY DRUMMOND

Blessed is the influence of
one true loving human soul on another.

GEORGE ELIOT

If at first you don't succeed,
do it like your teacher told you.